WOODWORKING FOR BEGINNERS

The Ultimate Woodworking Guide and Projects!

Darren Jones

Table of Contents

Introduction

I want to thank you and congratulate you for getting my book...

"Woodworking for Beginners"

This book will help you learn the basics of woodworking, from picking up the right tools to creating your first piece.

In this book, you will discover how easy it is for you to begin designing furniture and complete home improvement projects, even with zero woodworking background. This book will provide you everything that you need to know about selecting the right kind of wood, prepping your workshop, choosing the right finish for your wooden piece, and so much more.

This book is not only for beginners – it is also created to serve as a resource for those who are returning to this hobby and for people who are trying to improve their technique and troubleshoot their woodworking creations. This will serve as your comprehensive guide for woodworking.

Thanks again for purchasing this book, I hope you enjoy it!

CHAPTER 1

Getting to know Woodworking

As a person who just got recently interested in woodworking, you need to gain a lowdown on this hobby, so you can fully immerse yourself on what this activity is all about. Woodworking is a craft that asks but a few things from its pursuers:

Firstly, one needs creativity. Everyone is born with this trait, but a woodworker must develop a real desire to create using wood in order to fully appreciate this craft.

Secondly, craftsmen require patience and care to ensure the quality of their craft. This observance to properness produces woodwork of fine quality and helps develop and improve skill.

Lastly, you need the craftsman's tools. A woodworker would be lost without his most basic kit, which usually consists of his handsaw, pocket-knife and oilstone to sharpen his blades. A small assortment of wood scraps set aside to supplement whatever project you are making will also come in handy. However, this is not the complete set of basic tools a woodworker has to have, but the set that he absolutely must have in any situation.

Selecting Wood for Projects

Woodworking is, first and foremost, about choosing the right type of wood. Knowing what kind of wood best suits your project is a matter of familiarizing yourself with the properties of your different options. Knowing the type of wood stocks available in lumberyards and home improvement stores will help you identify what kind of wood piece you can work on as soon as possible.

When selecting the type of wood, you need to familiarize yourself with the following:

1. Hardwood

Hardwood is the typical stock that you would encounter and probably the type of wood that you would want to work on most of the time if you are interested in building furniture and other fine woodworking projects. However, keep in mind that the term "hardwood" does not really refer to the material's hardness, but actually refer to the species of the tree the word comes from.

Hardwood refers to wood sources from deciduous trees, or trees with broader leaves. In general, working hardwood is a lot harder than softwood, but of course there are some exceptions to this rule. For example, balsa is a soft and light material but falls under the classification of hardwood. Hardwood trees also tend to lose their leaves around winter and are preferred because of the variety of texture and colors that they offer.

Consider the following when you select hardwood stock:

a. The look of the finished piece

If you are going to do a paint job at the end of the project, then you don't want to waste your money buying hardwood that look better when stained. You should use poplar and other similar types of wood known for stability and ability to absorb paint. On the other hand, if you are looking to produce beautifully stained craft, you would want to go for wood with rich color, such as maple, mahogany, walnut, and oak.

b. Location

Think about how you intend to use the piece – do you want it placed inside your home, or do you plan to leave it outside as outdoor furniture? If you're looking to make outdoor furniture, you may want to select moisture-resistant wood such as cypress.

c. Weather effects on wood

One of the things that you need to always keep in mind when buying wood is how weather would affect the material when the season changes. Keep in mind that wood is bound to expand or contract based on moisture and temperature changes even after it has been assembled, so it's better to consider the type of climate in your area and how your wood stock would be affected by temperature and moisture.

2. Softwood

Softwood is found in abundance in home improvement stores, and that is for a good reason – softwood is cheaper, almost readily available in many locations in Europe and the US, and suitable to use in a lot of general projects for homes. While they definitely can be a bang for your buck, keep in mind that that does not make these materials ideal for everything that you need.

Softwood refers to the material you can harvest from evergreen or coniferous trees that grows in abundance in the northern hemisphere. These types of trees can be easily cultivated and normally produces straight trunks upon harvest, which makes excellent material for paper and fiberboard. When you go to a home improvement store, you would find that softwood is typically classified as the following:

a. SPF – an acronym which stands for spruce, pine, and fir. These woods are typically light-colored and the growth rings have wider spaces.

b. yellow pine – yellowish wood material made out of pine. Some people select this type of wood to get a natural yellowish stain.

When To Use Softwood?

Softwood is normally ideal for construction purposes, but they do not make good materials for furniture building. When you decide to use softwood for your project, you need to make sure that your material has already acclimatized to the environment you are using it in so that it would not make unwanted movement after assembly.

Softwoods are especially good for projects that involve painting such as cabinets and dog houses, but are not great if you want to get a stained wood effect on your finish product. They also do not look as aesthetic as hardwood as furniture and displays.

Beginner Woods

Beginners should start with a few pieces of smooth cedar, sugar pine, or basswood. These woods work for beginners well because they can quickly familiarize themselves with the woods' characteristics. Spending enough time familiarizing yourself with these woods will soon enable you to determine which kind best suits your needs upon sight.

Once you are familiar with the beginner woods' properties and the way they react when you cut and whittle them, you can move on to hard woods. Different woods work for different projects, though you will find that those that are ideal for beginners are useful for almost any project you aim to craft.

In any project, one must have pieces of wood that split straight and without a hitch. The said piece must be soft enough so as not to crack open ahead of the blade as it carves into the wood. Note that this can potentially ruin that piece. It also needs to be strong enough to maintain its integrity, even after having a big part of it carved off. If a piece of wood seems to be useless at the time, you would do well to save it, as it may be a good fit for something else. You would be surprised what one can do with the oddest blocks of wood and a little creativity.

Choosing and Examining Wood

When it comes to choosing wood, aside from determining whether the stock you are looking at is right for your project, you should look also look for defects. When examining the wood, the first parts you need to look at are the four sides. Any blemishes and imperfections in the wood caused by natural forces and milling problems are most obvious on these parts. However, not all defects can be harmful to your project, as some of them can give a certain feel and character to a piece. Of course, it would be up to you to consider whether the stock of wood that you have could still be used as material for your project.

Detecting Wood Warping

After you have ensured that the piece you are examining is usable, the next thing you should do is to check it for any signs of warping.

Bows are curved warps along the face of the piece. To detect bows, set the piece of stock up lengthwise by placing one end of the piece on the floor and holding it up. Afterwards, look down its long axis to determine if there is any deformation. Any curve that you see along the face is a bow. A piece with only one bow may be acceptable depending on usage, but it is advisable to steer clear from pieces with two or more bows.

Crooks are warps along the edge of the piece. The tree's growth naturally causes it. It is advisable to avoid pieces with crooks.

However, pieces with minor crooks can still be salvaged by cutting them into smaller pieces and leaving the defective pieces out of the project.

Winds appear as two ends of the wood warping in a twisted shape. You can detect this by setting a straight stick or meter along the length of the wood and sliding it along crosswise. Any deviation from the straight movement suggests evidence of winding. This is by far the most troublesome type of wood warping there is. It is important to avoid winding pieces, as these can compromise the integrity of your entire project, especially if used in crucial structural parts.

Cups are any curvatures along the width of the board. The worst kinds of cups are those in which both sides along the width of the wood curl up in a sort of convex shape. They are generally obvious, but checking using a straight instrument helps in detecting unnoticeable cups. Simple cupping can be fixed with surface planing, but any worse than that and it's not very useful for important structuring purposes. However, you can still use it for cosmetic purposes.

Additionally, you should check the dryness of the stock. Some woodworkers use portable moisture checkers for this purpose. However, simply asking an employee how long the wood has been in stock can help you determine its amount of moisture. Usually, newer wood has more moisture as it had much time adjusting to the local climate. If you do decide to buy newer wood, make sure that you let it sit for a couple of weeks before using it.

 Other things worth checking for are **cracks**, which can be the cause of fragility, as some of the smaller ones are caused by stress from the drying process. These cracks can worsen if the piece is not completely dry, and pieces that possess those characteristics should be avoided. You can still use relatively dry pieces that have a few minor cracks by cutting off the affected areas.

Your Workshop

As a craft that involves heavy tools and materials, you would need an adequate space to set all of your stuff, a place with enough storage space and wiggle room for working on your wood.

Some beginning woodworkers may think that they need a huge space to work, like a garage or warehouse. Having bigger workspaces does mean easier waste management and more room for tools and supplies. If you have that kind of space, then you will not run into too many problems to get your workshop up and running, and do not need much direction in this matter. However, while this is certainly necessary for large-scale projects, it has not necessarily required for woodworking.

Since setting up your workshop in larger spaces is not usually problematic, this part of the chapter aims at those who want to set up a workshop in a more compact space. This approach to woodworking is less convenient and requires a bit more effort and expenditure than having a larger workshop, but it is still entirely possible to work with what space you have.

Once you think you have found an adequate space to accommodate your wood supplies, workbench and tools, you will need to determine just how those things can fit in that space. You will need to consider everything, from the size of your projects to the quantity of your supplies to whether or not you are going to use power tools. In a generally cramped space, woodworking will be much easier if you cut your wood into smaller pieces. Employees at lumberyards provide this service, usually for a fee.

If your space is really cramped and you cannot manage to squeeze in any power tools, you would have to make do with hand tools. Alternatively, there are always smaller, portable bench-top and handheld power tools that are adequate for small-scale projects.

Another concern would be the ventilation and waste management. Unlike larger workspaces, smaller workshops need a good sawdust control system, preferably the more compact air filters specifically designed for smaller shops. Using dust masks while working also helps.

As for cleaning up waste, spending some time during work to gather sawdust helps control it from spreading. A much easier alternative is to cover your floors with laminate flooring and just shake off the sawdust at the end of the day. Additionally, surrounding yourself with some temporary walls can help prevent the sawdust from spreading outside your work area.

General Safety

As with every activity that involves handling sharp tools and heavy materials, safety comes first. For those only starting out in woodworking, this cannot be stressed heavily enough. Those who lack experience cannot simply settle on the thought that "it won't happen to me". New woodworkers should learn about these safety guidelines, so they will have a safer and more enjoyable experience.

1. **Wear appropriate clothing and safety equipment.**

   Wearing safety glasses and latex gloves can save you from getting wood chips in your eyes and a nasty splinter. The gloves are also necessary when you work with wood treating chemicals such as finishes. If you are working with noisy tools, it is advisable to wear hearing protection. Do not wear loose-fitting clothes, and remove any dangling articles of clothing as they might get caught in saw blades.

2. Stay sober.

Just as you cannot drive under the influence, you cannot handle sharp instruments under the influence as well. Note that you are still a beginner in woodworking, so stay sober when working on a project to prevent any untoward accidents.

3. Unplug every tool after use.

This way, you cannot accidentally set off a power tool that you do not need to, when you least expect it. A good way to enforce this rule is to use only one extension cord for all of your 110-volt power tools. That way, you would have to unplug your tool from the extension cord before you can use another one.

4. Always keep your tools sharp.

Dull tools are inefficient. You need to exert more effort to use them. They also produce very rough cuts. Sharpening your tools and cleaning them regularly can help produce cleaner cuts, and are less likely to bind into the material or kick back at you, which is a common cause of injury. Additionally, check for any metal objects that may obstruct the path of your cutting tool, as this can cause damage to it.

5. Never put your body near a blade that is still spinning.

This is an important rule to observe, especially when you are changing bits or blades on a power tool. You do not want your power saw's blades spinning at 5800 rpm as you are trying to jam your hand in the assembly to change its blade. Rule # 3 is very important in observing this rule. Unplug the power tool first before trying to replace any part of it.

Always wait for the blade to stop before you try to put any part of your body near it. If you absolutely must do something that involves putting your hand near the blade; say, pushing waste and cut-offs away from the blade, use a piece of scrap or a stick to do so.

6. **Consider the tool you are using as the most dangerous tool.**

There is a possibility of injury from any tool in your shed, and injuries typically occur not because of tools carelessly strewn around but during usage. For this reason, handle very tool with care, even if they are merely hand tools. Always return them to a secure area, or their corresponding case, when done using them.

CHAPTER 2

Tools of the Trade

The Craftsman's Toolkit

Every woodworker has different needs and preferences; hence, they all need a different set of tools. However, seasoned woodworkers' tool inventories have changed and grown since they first started out, out of necessity and experience. Since beginners do not have much of both, they will only need to buy the standard and basic kit to start woodworking. Expand your toolset as your skills develop and your needs become more complex.

When buying tools, it is a good rule to conduct an extensive research. Do not rush yourself when building your inventory. Shop carefully and be on the hunt for sales and specials. Reading woodworking magazines and catalogs can also help you find the best deal for your tools.

Additionally, buying the best quality tools that you can afford is the most feasible choice, as good tools don't really deteriorate in quality even after a lifetime of use, with basic maintenance, of course. Manufacturers usually offer products for both hobbyists and industrial users. The former is generally inexpensive, and the latter is more heavy-duty. See to it that the tools you buy match your needs.

Basic Woodworking Tools

The Hammer

Every woodworker knows this one. Contrary to what many beginners might think, woodworkers need more than one hammer to suit all the different kinds of projects they might want to undertake. Claw hammers are mainly used for nailing, tack hammers are used to start carpet tacks, carpenter's hammers are used for general hammering, etc.

When selecting a hammer, you would want it to consider the following:

1. Weight

Weight is indispensible to hammers since the heaviness of this tool would determine how easy it would be to drive nails into the wood. As a rule of thumb, it is best to acquire a hammer with a weight of about 20 ounces to be able to drive large nails into any type of wood and still be limber enough to remove broken or bent fasteners easily.

2. Handle

Pulling nails using the claw may cause a strain on your hand and on the handle of the tool. If you are going to work on a lot of woodworking, you can expect that you would be pulling a lot of nails, so make sure that the hammer's handle is made up of tougher material such as steel or fiberglass. To protect your hands and to pull out materials easily, invest in a hammer with rubber or vinyl grip.

However, if you have projects that do not require you to pull out a lot of nails, then you would want to use a traditional adze-eye hammer fitted with a hickory handle. Hickory is one of the best materials when it comes to vibration absorption and would do the trick in reducing hand and wrist stress when driving nails.

3. Head

There are two types of hammer heads – the waffle head and the finish head. The waffle head is the one that has grooves and this type of hammer is ideal for driving nails into the wood when a smooth finish in the wood is not your concern. Since hammers with waffle heads are designed for just driving in nails faster, make sure that you don't use them if you do not want indentation marks on your stocks.

Finish head hammers are great for driving smaller nails for finishing purposes. These heads are slightly rounded and smooth, which is ideal to use on wood that would serve as covers for foundations.

The Pocket Knife

This is a versatile tool that you should consider bringing with you when working on projects. This knife would be ideal in cutting off thin materials and dealing with mortises, and even with scoring the stock wood before making a cut or driving in a nail.

It is advisable to keep two of these knives, one heavier and larger to take care of heavy cutting and trimming, and one for general whittling purposes. Maintain their good condition to increase their lifespan. This gives you the chance to use them for a long time. If you do not have a pocket knife, or you do not want to ruin yours while woodworking, you may want to invest instead on a utility knife with reversible and disposable blades.

The Mallet

Mallets are hammer-like tools made for handwork and assembling wooden parts. Heavier mallets are made out of dense hardwood, like maple or poplar, and are used for heavy work. Carver's mallets are smaller tools, usually made out of wood, but sometimes have its head capped with brass.

Other mallets, like rubber mallets and dead blow hammers are good for delivering strong blows but without marring soft surfaces. These are also useful in hammering together soft and delicate pieces of wood.

The Chisel

You can use this tool to chop, pare and carve wood into your desired shape. The best chisel sizes for beginners are ¼, ½, ¾, and 1-inch. Note that you need to keep the chisels sharp so you can use them properly. Choose chisels that are comfortable to hold and learn the basics of sharpening them. To sharpen this tool, you need a sharpening stone and a honing guide.

When using the chisel, you will need to work from the front of your piece so that you can distribute weight evenly and distribute your weight right on the handle to ease the tool right into the wood. If you need extra force, you can use the heel of your hand to strike the chisel handle's butt on a downward manner. If you need a lot more, which is usually the case when dealing with hardwood, you can use a wooden mallet to tap the chisel's butt. Never use a steel-headed hammer for forcing the chisel into the wood, as this may cause damage to your tools.

Screwdrivers

Screwdrivers are designed to drive and remove screws. Since there are projects that may require you disassemble pieces for easier movement or repair, it is very important that you have a set of screwdrivers with different sizes (recognized according to number) and shapes right in your toolbox.

Here are the screwdrivers that you may want to stock in for different purposes:

1. Philips – characterized by the X tip, these screwdrivers are typically used for drywall, deck, machine, and other types of screws that have the X head.

2. Flathead – these screwdrivers has spade-like flat tips that are typically used to drive and remove screws from most woods.

3. Square – marked by the square tip, these screwdrivers are designed to drive and remove square head screws that are commonly used in furniture. Square head screws are less prone to stripping than Philips and flatheads.

Nail Sets

Nail sets are used to drive nails beneath or flush the surface of the wood stock. These tools look like round-headed chisels, which serve to tap the nail the rest of the way to prevent denting the wood with the hammer. Nail sets are available according to the size of the nails that you are using, so it would be advisable to keep stock of different sizes.

The Hand Plane

Hand planes can help smoothen a rough board and adjust its thickness. Nowadays, it is already possible to replace hand planes with wood sanders when dimensioning wood. However, this does not mean that hand planes are obsolete. If well honed, a hand plane can finish dimensioning wood in a few minutes, whereas a sander may take more than an hour. Compared to sanders, hand planes produce much smoother surfaces, and they do so without producing an unpleasant cloud of sawdust. Like chisels, however, they also need a bit of preparation before you can set them to work

The Hand Saw

This tool is still very reliable in this age of power saws, and a woodcraftsman absolutely must have it on hand at all times. For beginners, a coping saw for general cutting and shaping should suffice.

The Clamps

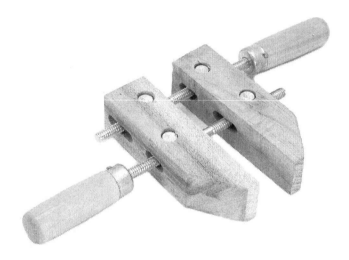

This tool is indispensable for woodworkers, since it stops your wood from moving too much as you work on it. Clamps are bought in pairs, and any beginner would need at least one pair of 24-inch bar clamps. That is just the bare minimum, and you are very much encouraged to buy more clamps. In woodworking, you can never have enough of these things.

The Workbench

While not exactly considered a "tool" by most people, workbenches are probably the most indispensable item not only in woodworking, but also in any other craft. A well-designed workbench can maximize convenience and efficiency for the woodworker.

When purchasing or building your own workbench, you only have a few goals to meet, which are the following:

1. It has to have the right height

A good height is somewhere between your thigh and waist. You do not need to agonize too much on meeting the perfect height since you would adapt to your bench's height when you start working on it frequently.

2. It has to be sturdy

A good workbench can be anything that is heavy enough and dry. While most woodworkers would require their workbench to be made out of hardwood top, but that is not necessary. As long as it is flat, wobbly, and sturdy enough to work on, it is fine.

3. It has to be large enough

The size of your workbench would depend on the size of your project, so it may be wise to build a couple or more of these when you intend to work on multiple pieces. If you do not have a large woodshop, then it is only fitting to build a workbench that is proportional to the size of your workspace.

Project Layout Tools

For this section of woodworking tools, you generally need only three tools:

25-inch tape measure/ steel rule/ folding rule

12-inch combination square

.005 drafting pen

The three tools can actually fulfill most of your measuring and lay-outing needs. As for the first measuring tool mentioned, each variant has its own strengths and weaknesses, and you should pick one that best suits your needs and preferences. However, getting all of them is advisable if you want to be really successful in this craft.

The **tape measure** can measure long distances without the inconvenience of having to use a folding ruler. When you buy a tape measure, make sure that it has the metric system on one side, and the standard system on the other. This would make you compute measurements faster without having to make conversions. One major disadvantage of this is that the hook at the end of the tape can be a cause for inaccuracy sometimes.

The **folding rule** does not have the tape measure's hook disadvantage. It combines a large measuring range with accuracy, and even has a built-in sliding rule to measure interior distances and depth. The biggest downside to it is its size, which makes it a little difficult to set up and use.

Though only good for small measurements of 6 inches or less, **steel rules** combine the accuracy of the folding rule and the compact size of the tape measure.

The **Combination Square**, also known as the layout square, helps you draw perpendicular lines. It also allows for the drawing of 45-degree lines, finding the center of wooden boards, and transferring measurements, especially when you are about to make a cut on a table square and you want to determine the angle for the miter or the bevel. This versatile tool is very vital to woodworking as well. As such, it is advisable to get the best one you can buy.

As for marking, the **.005 Drafting Pen** is most suitable because using it for marking purposes is hassle-free. It can clearly mark certain parts of the wood. Just make sure to marks only once, as doing it twice can lead to inaccuracy.

Power Tools

As an aspiring woodworker, you need to gather a few power tools. You can use these tools in woodworking, but with a little more finesse and accuracy. Beginners who have little experience in power tools should use them sparingly and only after becoming comfortable with hand tools. This part of the chapter will concentrate on the simpler power tools that are easier for beginners to use and familiarize themselves with.

The Drill

This bores holes in the wood for multiple purposes. The real importance in this lies in its various bits. The standard twist bit is good for general drilling, although it leaves a rough hole. The spur bit is friendlier to wood and leaves much smoother holes. Auger bits can make deeper, straighter holes, usually up to five feet deep. Beginners should read up on the different bits before trying them out.

When looking for a drill, it's crucial to take a good look at the features that different brands and models have to offer instead of relying on brand popularity alone. You would want to invest in a drill that has variable speeds, reversible action, keyless chuck, and a comfortable grip.

You might also see that there are cordless drills available on the market, but a lot of expert woodworkers advise against buying them over corded ones. The reason is that drilling consumes too much power which may immediately drain the tool's battery. As a result, many manufacturers compromise features, such as additional speeds, in order to preserve battery life in their product.

The Power Saw

There are many different types of power saws, suited for different kinds of work. Here are the saws that you may want to invest in:

- Circular saws are designed for straight-line cutting, and also have the power to crosscut and rip through different materials apart from wood.

  When buying circular saws, the rule of thumb is that bigger saws usually have better power, which makes it ideal to buy models that have higher horsepower than brands that offer the same size. You may also want to check out how the saw can be controlled for adjustments when you want to hold it at a different angle and if it has an anti-locking clutch, which will allow the blade to slip when it gets stuck in the wood to protect the motor.

- Jigsaws are ideal in cutting curves and shapes into the wood. When you use the jigsaw, you can move around the stock that you intend to cut around the table while the jigsaw is turned on to cut on a specific angle or stock part.

Many jigsaws are able to cut up to a maximum of two inches of depth for most woodworking purposes and about ½ inch on metal material. Some jigsaws may offer deeper cuts, but you may not want to opt for them since the deeper the blade is into your material, the higher the chance that the blade would bend and break.

When buying a jigsaw, you may want to look for higher-end models that have the variable speed and orbital action features, which would allow you to cut materials other than wood. At the same time, orbital action also allows you to switch the angle of the blade so you can adjust it according to the material that you intend to cut. By switching the angle, you can obtain a smoother cut that may keep the wood's splintering to a minimum.

Beginners can find out what each type of saw does as they gain experience, but for those starting out, a standard circular saw or table saw is the way to go.

The Sander

This eliminates the need for manual sanding, so expect to be able to save time when using this. Belt sanders sand in only one direction. You can also use it only in the direction of the grain. Orbital sanders, on the other hand, can work in any direction. However, they leave tiny circular scratches on the wood. Random orbit sanders eliminate the circular scratches found in orbital sanders.

Buying Secondhand Tools

Since you are just starting out with woodworking, it is possible that you do not have the budget yet to buy all the tools that you need, especially if you desire power tools in your shop. However, budget should not stop you from getting the tools that you need when you are eager to start with a woodworking project.

Follow this guide to buy pre-owned tools to get the right equipment at a bargain:

1. As much as possible, go for reputable brands

A good Google search will show you what brands are worth purchasing since they boast longevity and adaptability to different crafting situations. As much as possible, avoid buying brands that have poor reviews, even though they carry a cheap price tag.

2. Ask why the tool is for sale

You have the opportunity to shop around for secondhand tools since it is very likely that you would encounter fellow woodworkers that have switched to a different tool or think that their stuff are just collecting dust in their garage. When you shop around, always ask for the reason why they have decided to sell the tool. This would give you hints on possible problems on the tool that they want out of their shop.

3. Test before buying

Whether buying a new or secondhand tool, never shell out cash for something that you have not seen or tested. It may be a little difficult if the person you are buying from is far from you, but resist making a deal over emails and phone calls even if the tool seems to be a steal.

Once you see the tool, make sure that it is working properly. Check for safety features and look out for any possible signs of damage. If it is your first time handling the tool, you may also want to check if the owner still has the manual or any other document that came with the tool.

Ask the owner if you can use the tool. You may also want to bring a couple of stock wood that you have in order to test the tool the way you intend to use it in your shop.

4. Negotiate for a fair price

Once you feel that you are ready to buy the tool, negotiate with the owner if it is still possible to lower the price. You can bring up any possible issues that you have seen on the tool, such as dings and scratches, to lower down the price. You can also point out that even though scratches will not affect the performance of the tool, it can still be a sign of possible abuse.

Of course, make sure that you haggle for a price that is fair to you and the owner. Look up for the original price of the tool and compare the owner's price to other secondhand offers with the same model.

CHAPTER 3

Creating Your Woodshop

Now that you know the tools and the type of wood stock that you need to get for your projects, it's time to start creating your work space.

Characteristics of a Good Shop

You know you have the right space for working when your woodshop meets the following criteria:

1. Plenty of space

Your shop needs to have plenty of space to accommodate your workbenches (you would probably need more than two of these), tools (powered or not), and your wood stock. You need to have the right amount of space to store and maneuver large stocks in your shop and see to it that moving from one tool to another doesn't make you bump into working tables and large powered tools.

2. Connectivity to sources of electricity

You are very likely to use powered tools, even if you are working on smaller pieces. While there are plenty of battery powered tools out there nowadays, you would still need to make sure that there are enough electric sockets in your shop that allows you to use multiple tools simultaneously. It also follows that your electric sockets have the right wattage for your tools.

3. Ample lighting

Lighting is everything in a woodshop – working under poor lighting is not only extremely unsafe, it also runs the risk of creating errors in your design.

4. Proper ventilation

You need to protect yourself from fumes when you are working with wood, especially since you will work at your workpiece using stains, paints, and adhesives. Make sure that your woodshop has enough ventilation to help circulate the air and prevent noxious fumes from getting trapped in your workshop.

5. Good insulation

Your woodshop needs to be equipped with proper insulation in order to protect your tools and wood stock from moisture and temperature changes. Prevent any risk of rust accumulation, power supply damage, or warping of stocks by making sure that your woodshop is dry.

6. Good organization system

A safe woodshop is organized. By keeping woodshop items in an organized fashion, you would be aware of any damage that tools and stock have incurred over time and enable you to reach items that you need safely. An organized woodshop would also enable you to easily see which items you need to replenish or repair, apart from letting you move around your work area efficiently.

Working with What You Have

Since you are just starting out with woodworking, it would be unlikely that you automatically have a large, climate-controlled space at home to hold all your tools. It is also unlikely that you have the space to build large weatherproof cabinets to store powered tools and stocks. However, that should not prevent you from getting started right away with woodworking.

These tips would allow you to optimize your work space and help you keep your woodshop safe and efficient.

1. Invest in dehumidifiers

If you cannot install air conditioning or heating in your workshop, then dehumidifiers would do the trick in keeping your tools and supply dry. If you think that a couple of dehumidifiers are not enough, you can also use silica gel packets to help your stored items remain safe from humidity.

2. Optimize lighting

It is important that you buy lightning equipment that allows light to spread in the entire work area and not just on a particular spot in the woodshop. When that is not possible, make sure that you have ample lighting in the spot that you frequently use. You may also want to paint your shop's walls white to get a better bounce of lighting across the room. To help with the illumination, make sure that your space has provisions for natural lighting.

If you find that the available light would not be sufficient to illuminate a spot that contains a tool that is difficult to move, then you may want to install focused lighting over this area. Make sure those lamps for focused lighting lean towards the spot that you are working on to prevent shadows. To help with the illumination on pieces that you are working on, you can also equip some of your tools with small on-tool lights for supplementary lighting.

3. Use original boxes for storage

If you do not have a weatherproof space to store your power tools, consider keeping them in their original cases or boxes. These cases are designed to prevent humidity from reaching your tools while protecting them from physical damage.

4. Store only what you can use

If you do not have much space for a woodshop, consider buying only what you need to prevent any organization troubles and to allow you to move easily within that space. If you are not likely to use large powered tools like table or circular saws, don't buy them until you get a bigger spot for your shop. Avoid storing large wood stocks until they become necessary for your project.

5. Install pegboards

Pegboards are inexpensive, easy to assemble, and great for organizing hand tools and supplies that you always reach for. Since they are commonly installed right on the wall, these storage helpers would not cost you any floor space.

Top Woodshop Accessories

At this point, you would also want to get your hands on woodshop accessories that are designed to make work easier and more efficient. Here are some of the woodshop accessories that you may like to have:

1. Portable shop table

This accessory is great for people who do not have enough space on their workbench and tables, but also don't have enough floor space to accommodate another large table. If such a situation applies to you, you may want to build a table with casters that allows you to fold your table away and also allow the table legs to be secured to the floor when you need to work on it.

2. Bench with vise

This is probable one of the handiest accessories that you would like to have in your woodshop. With this workbench, you can have a series of holes in your working spot that would allow you to move the vise to another hole to fit the piece that you are working on.

3. Sawhorses

Sawhorses are accessories that you are going to need sooner than you think, since you are bound to cut wood. These accessories are also great for stacking up wood stocks.

4. Clamps

Clamps are the woodworker's best friend, since they are accessories that you can fit on mostly any workbench or table that are designed to keep a stock still while you are working on it. As a woodworking axiom states, you can never have enough of these accessories when you start to build.

5. Vacuums or dust collectors

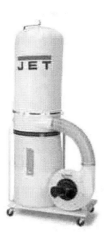

You can expect that you are going to accumulate wood dust in your shop. In order to protect your tools and make it safe for you to work in your shop, you would need to invest in dust collectors or vacuums.

6. Bench grinder

Some people think that bench grinders are not woodworking tools, and you can assume that they are correct. However, bench grinders are efficient tools for a good number of shop tasks, especially in keeping tools sharp.

7. Jigs

Jigs are tools that you can create in order to help you cut wood into certain shapes. You would want to stock up on these tools especially when you plan to make tables and furniture sets.

8. Featherboards

A featherboard is a tool that you use on the router table or table saw in order to hold small pieces of wood against the blade to produce a clean cut. You can hold it with a clamp on the table or workbench while the blade runs past the stock that you want to cut.

CHAPTER 4

Choosing Boards

When you get to the lumberyard to choose boards for your project, you will realize that not all boards are the same. When choosing the board type for your project, there are three types of boards to choose from, which are categorized according to how the growth rings of the tree that they came from relate to the wide side, or the face, of the board.

Why Growth Rings Matter

Growth rings, and their relationship to the face of the board, tell you about the overall stability of the wood. That means that depending on how these growth rings appear on the board that you intend the purchase, the wood that you are going to buy would move according to your location's humidity. As a rule of thumb, the movement that a piece of wood tends to make depends on the angle of the growth rings against the board's face - the lower the angle of the growth rings in relation to the face of the board, the more movement the board will possibly make.

Cuts in Wood Flooring

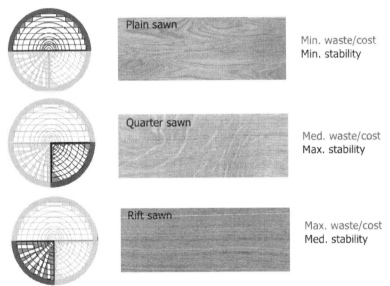

Plain sawn — Min. waste/cost / Min. stability

Quarter sawn — Med. waste/cost / Max. stability

Rift sawn — Max. waste/cost / Med. stability

1. Plain-sawn boards

These boards are the most common type of board that you would encounter in the lumberyard. If you do not ask for a type of cut in a lumberyard, the salesman you are talking to will automatically assume that you want to get this type of board. These are also the cheapest board type that you can purchase.

Plain-sawn boards are marked by growth rings appear less than 30° on the board's face. Since the grains run against the board in an angle close to its face, this type of board is more likely to cup or warp – it can make as much movement as ¼ when the climate in your area gets wetter or drier. However, it does not mean that the wood is not usable at all for your project – all you need is to cut sections that seem to be unstable for your project.

2. Rift-sawn boards

These boards are characterized by its growth rings that meet the face at about 30° to 60°. You will see that these boards have straight grain patterns, compared to the plain-sawn wood's circular pattern. Because of how these grains appear, they offer better stability to your piece (moving only as much as 1/8 inch, depending on your area's climate), although they costs about 50% more than the price of the plain-sawn board.

3. Quarter-sawn boards

These boards are characterized by growth rights that grow equal to or more than 60° from the board's face. These boards have grains that form a straight pattern that creates a ribbon-like or flake-like appearance on the wood.

Quarter-sawn boards are the most stable as they make almost no discernible movement over time. However, quality means that you have to pay the price – these boards are also the most expensive among the board options available in the lumberyard. However, they are the best type of boards to use in Mission-style and most sophisticated projects.

When you want to select a board for any type of project, you need to consider the amount that you are willing to spend for the wood, as well as the availability of the species that you want to take the boards from. You also would need the aesthetics that you want to achieve in your design. However, it doesn't mean that your woodworking projects should be severely influenced by the wood's availability. Over time, you would be able to create pieces that have enough stability and aesthetic, as long as you have a great plan on how to cut and prepare the material that you have available.

CHAPTER 5

Working with Sheet Goods

Sheet goods refer to the different wood products that are available in most home improvement stores when it is difficult for you to find standard lumber. They are also products that are better to use in some furniture projects that you may have in mind. For example, plywood would be better to use than dimensional lumber in creating cabinets.

While sheet goods are easier to find and are considerably easier on the budget, you would need to pay attention on how you are going to store and use them for your projects. Not all sheet goods provide you with the same amount of stability, which means that you need to buy the material that works well with your project design and use.

Using Plywood

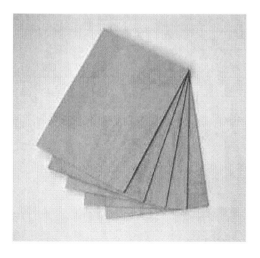

Plywood is most likely the most versatile and popular manmade material for woodworking. This sheet good is made up of thin strips of wood glued and laminated together until they become stable and strong sheets. Because of this, plywood is less prone to shrinkage and expansion. However, while it doesn't shrink or expand along the grain, they are likely to split with the grain.

When you pay attention to furniture made out of plywood, you will notice that a side of the plywood is more solid, and the other side is rough. If you want to avoid having to sand the rough surface, there are plywood boards that are sold with two solid faces, but are considerably more expensive. You may also notice that there are lumber yards or home improvement centers that are selling hardwood plywood, which looks like they are made out of cherry, oak, or birch. However, these woods are not made up of entirely hardwood – underneath the surface are sheets of SPF. For this reason, you may not want to sand the surface of such plywood thoroughly to avoid exposing the non-hardwood layer.

Medium Density Fiberboard (MDF) and Particle Boards

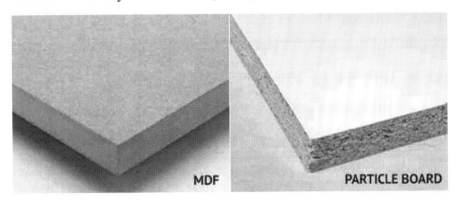

MDF materials are considerably cheaper than real wood. It is made up of different parts of wood pulp, mostly from logs that are not selected by lumber yards. The wood from these logs are reduced into fine chips that are mixed with resin and wax, and then pressed into boards. After the board is dried, they are laminated and trimmed to be sold at a price much lower than the wood that they are trying to resemble.

MDFs resemble particle boards, which is essentially created using the same process. MDFs, however, are denser since the wood particles within them are more compact, which makes it a better replacement for plywood.

While these materials have perfect dimensions, machines very well, and has no knots, using these material can have these disadvantages:

1. doesn't hold screws and other types of mechanical fasteners as well as grained lumber

2. they cannot be routed well and can dull blades faster

3. requires pilot holes to prevent splitting when attaching nails or screws

4. very susceptible to water damage

5. dust contains chemicals that are dangerous to breathe in

CHAPTER 6

Using the Right Stocks and Tools for the Job

Now that you have your woodshop ready, it's time for you to get to work. In order to create your first piece, here are some beginners techniques that you would want to learn:

Getting Wood Sizes Right

New and Old Standard Lumber Sizes

Lumber Classification	Nominal Size Thickness	Width	Actual S4S Size Thickness	Width	Old S4S Size Thickness	Width
Dimension	2"	4"	1½"	3½"	1⅝"	3⅝"
	2"	6"	1½"	5½"	1⅝"	5⅝"
	2"	8"	1½"	7¼"	1⅝"	7½"
	2"	10"	1½"	9¼"	1⅝"	9½"
	2"	12"	1½"	11¼"	1⅝"	11½"
Timbers	4"	6"	3½"	5½"	3⅝"	5⅝"
	4"	8"	3½"	7¼"	3⅝"	7½"
	4"	10"	3½"	9¼"	3⅝"	9½"
	6"	6"	5½"	5½"	5⅝"	5⅝"
	6"	8"	5½"	7¼"	5⅝"	7½"
	6"	10"	5½"	9¼"	5⅝"	9½"
	8"	8"	7¼"	7¼"	7½"	7½"
	10"	10"	9¼"	9¼"	9½"	9½"
Common Boards	1"	4"	¾"	3½"	25/32"	3⅝"
	1"	6"	¾"	5½"	25/32"	5⅝"
	1"	8"	¾"	7½"	25/32"	7⅝"
	1"	10"	¾"	9¼"	25/32"	9½"
	1"	12"	¾"	11¼"	25/32"	11½"

When you visit a local store to purchase wood stock, you will notice that hardwood stocks are sold according to board foot, while softwood sizes come differently. While you may be working on projects that have exact sizing requirements, the board that you intend to buy may come in a different size than what is written on the display. The reason is that the size that you are going to get would depend on how the material on stock is milled and dried. Since wood can shrink when it is dried and milled, you get only ¾" when you are purchasing a 1" piece.

When purchasing stocks, keep these rules in mind:

1. Softwood sizing

Softwood is generally sold for general purpose woodworking and would normally come in 1x and 2x sizes. Softwoods are typically cut in uniform sizes and are stacked in the same manner in the lumber yard.

2. Hardwood sizing

Sizes for hardwood can be a lot trickier since it would depend on how the stock is surfaced. For this reason, you may get different dimensions depending on the surface side that you are looking at. Since hardwoods are sold according to board feet, you would want to keep in mind that a board foot is 12"x12"x1", or 1/12 of a cubic foot.

3. Plywood

Plywood is sold according to thickness and in 4'x8' sheets. It also comes according to grades, which depends on the sanded finish on the wood's surface. Grade A plywood is the smoothest and is sanded on both sides. You may also encounter plywood sheets that as graded as BC, meaning that one side of the wood is Grade B, while the other side is graded as C. Take note that when you sand the board's surface you may lose the thickness that you need for your project. Better opt for the Grade A plywood if you want your board to be close to the measurement that you have in mind.

Getting The Right Cut

When you are trying to cut wood, there is a variety of tools you may use. However, not all saws are the same. Saws have different effects on the wood and some have certain advantages over others. Keep the following in mind when you are making cuts:

1. Hand saws

Hand saws are your best option when you are trying to make quick cuts but you do not need them to be perfectly straight. While you need to exert effort in cutting using these tools, they are still the best to use when you need to get the job done fast. Take note that you cannot use a hand saw for wood when you are trying to cut metal – you need a different saw for that.

2. Jigsaw

Jigsaws are the best to use when you need to cut curves and shapes, however, this tool's reciprocating blade is not designed to create perfectly straight cuts. Remember that the blade of this tool can be replaced quickly if you need to cut a different material.

3. Circular saws

Circular saws are heavy duty and the best tool to use if you need to make long, straight cuts. Keep in mind that these power tools can be dangerous for beginners, but if you intend to do woodworking for a long time, investing in a circular saw would be a good thing to do.

Selecting Screws

When you want to connect two pieces of material, screws can be a better option than nails. However, the right screw would depend on the material that you want to connect. Here are some of the most common screws and when to use them.

a. Wood screws

These screws are characterized by unthreaded bit between the tip and the head (also known as shank), flat head, and a coarse pitch. The coarse pitch allows the screw to tap into the wood for a better connection. The unthread shank makes it possible for the screw to get flush when you drill it into the wood. When using these screws, remember that you need to make a pilot hole, which means that you need to drill the wood before screwing in.

b. Drywall screws

These screws also have unthreaded shanks and are longer than wood screws. It would also be a good idea to make a pilot hole into the wood before screwing them in.

c. Machine screws

These screws have fine threads and are stronger than other screws. You would normally secure them using a nut or a bolt.

d. Sheet metal screws

These self-tapping screws have a fine pitch and they have threads all the way to the head. They are a lot shorter than wood screws since they are not intended to go through thick material.

How long and wide should your screws be? Typically, screws are measured in gauge sizes – the higher the gauge is, the larger the diameter of the screw would be. For typical woodworking, you are more likely to use #6 to #12 gauges. If you want to purchase screws and stock them for general applications, you would want to buy #8 gauges.

The length of the screw would depend on the thickness and orientation of the pieces that you want to join together. As a rule, it would be ideal to select screws that are 2 or 3 times the thickness of the parts you want to attach. If you want to join a drawer that has ¼" thickness, you need to use a ¾" screw. However, keep in mind that longer screws mean that you need to drill the pilot deep enough. Make sure that when you do, you drill straight so that the screw won't come out farther into the wood.

Beginner Tips on Sanding

When you are working with wood, you can expect that your cuts and drill holes would make splinters and burs. The best way to deal with these imperfection is to sand the wood. Follow these tips to sand wood more efficiently.

1. Choose the right sandpaper

Sandpaper is used in all types of sanding equipment and it is important that you select the right grit to avoid damaging the wood or to get the finish that you want. Grits are normally determined by the number attached with them, with 20 being the coarsest and 1000 the finest. When you select sandpaper, you would want to choose coarse ones when you need to remove a lot of material. You also need to move to a finer grit for finishing. A 200 sandpaper is typically used for most finishing purposes.

2. Choose the right equipment

The sanding tool that you need to use would depend on the size of material that you need to finish. Here are the tools that you may want to invest in:

a. Hand sander

A hand sander is made up of a handle and a plate that allows you to attach sandpaper under it. You can use a hand sander if you need to sand a small flat piece.

b. Orbital sander

Orbital sanders have sanding disks and are ideal to use when you need to sand tight spaces and crevices. They are also ideal to use when sanding small electronics.

c. Belt sander

Belt sanders are powerful and make use of sandpaper belts to remove a lot of material. They are extremely useful when you need to sand a large flat surface.

Painting Tips

Once you have built your piece, you can choose to paint it for better protection and to improve its look. There are two types of pain that are commonly used for woodworking:

1. Latex

Latex is water based and is used in most general paint jobs. Latex is also easier to clean up and easier to apply on most wood surfaces. Latex paint is weather resistant and will adhere to most types of material.

2. Oil based

This type of paint adheres better to wood and is ideally applied over a previous coat of an oil-based paint. The disadvantage to using this paint is that you would need to use mineral oil or paint thinner to remove it from the surface you want to clean up.

Once you have chosen the paint, you need to select the sheen or glossiness level. Observe these rules to select the right amount of sheen for your paint:

1. Flat paint makes it possible for you to make seamless touch ups. It is also ideal to use when you want to hide imperfections on wood.

2. Glossier finish is more durable and weather-resistant.

3. It is easier to scrub or wash the surface of your piece when you select a glossier paint.

CHAPTER 7

Developing Your Woodshop Skills

At this point, you might have acquired the basic tools that you need to start building projects and you might have your first piece that you want to create out of your wood stock. By having the right skills in woodworking, you would be able to craft a fine piece of furniture without having to spend so much for advanced woodworking tools.

Here are skills that you need to master to ensure that you are going to make a solid and perfect craft whenever you head towards the woodshop:

1. Use the handsaw accurately

While the handsaw can be an easy tool to use, it is a tool that can break when used on the wrong material. There are saws that specialize in making the rip cut, or the type of cut that slices along with the grain of the wood, and the cross cut, which slices against the grain. That means that you may need to buy saws that are sharpened and filed differently to make them more efficient in cutting different types of wood.

Now, follow these steps to make sure that you are using the handsaw properly:

a. Hold the saw properly.

Hold the handsaw's handle with a pistol hand – your index finger should be pointing towards the direction you intend to make a cut. Your bicep and your elbow should also be in line with your index finger and the rest of the saw.

Your body needs to be positioned in such a way that you can comfortably move the arm holding the saw back and forth along the line you have marked to make the cut. Use the thumb of the hand that is not holding the saw right on the mark where the tip of the saw meets the line that you need to cut. Push the saw and draw it back gently to launch the blade into the wood. Remember to use the whole saw blade in cutting.

Grip the saw comfortably and make sure to apply just the right tension. When you grip it too loosely, you may not be able to apply the right pressure into the arm and the saw would not budge at all. However, if you grip it too tightly, then you may lose control of direction the blade.

b. Hold the piece appropriately.

Make sure that the board that you want to cut is clamped down on your workbench or sawhorses securely. This way, you would prevent your workpiece, and your saw, from slipping.

If your board is not held securely, your board will chatter or vibrate so much while the saw is trying to make the cut, which will make the wander off the line that you want to cut. To prevent that from happening, hold down the workpiece with a clamp that would hold the wood tightly and provide you with the opposing force that you need.

c. Lubricate, if needed.

To make the saw glide effortlessly as it makes the cut, you can apply some wax, such as burnt tea candles, to the sawplate. Doing so will help you protect the blade and keep your sawblade cool while making cuts. When you are done using your handsaw, wipe off the sawdust on the blade and wipe the handle and the sawblade with oil. This will condition the wood material of the handle and prevent the blade from rusting.

2. Cut large sheet goods accurately

Because you are more likely to work with sheet goods for most of your household woodworking needs, among the first skills that you need to learn is how to cut these types of wood accurately. However, it may be difficult to cut them right on top of your workbench. The trick to making a precise cut is to make an 8' straightedge using your circular saw. Do this by following these steps:

a. Rough-cut a board in half or put two sheets on top of each other and use the top board's factory edge serve as your straightedge when you rip off a wide strip of about 7" wide on the lower sheet. Afterwards, adjust the top boards edge to rip another 16"-wide strip on the bottom sheet.

b. Unplug the saw and measure from the blade to the edge of its base that you would find underneath the motor. Allow an additional 1" to this measurement and then attach the 7" strip to the 16" strip with a screw using the dimensions that you just measured.

c. Firmly place the saw's base against the edge of the upper wood strip and then cut away the excess on the lower wood strip. Support the piece of the wood that you are cutting off to prevent the saw from binding. Put a label on the straight edge that has the sawn side.

d. Clamp the edge of the base onto the marked cutline when you are ready to cut the wood. Run the edge of the base that you have marked to guide you while making the cut.

3. Gap-Free Gluing for Joint Boards

No boards are straight enough for to give you an edge-glue with zero gaps. You need to make sure that edges are straight in order to make a glue joint as strong as possible. To make sure that the edges of your stock wood are as true to the measure as possible for perfect glue joints, use the straight guide that you have made in the previous skill as your router guide to straighten the boards that you want to use as pieces of the joints using a spiral bit or a 1/2 straight bit.

a. Measure the distance from the router's base edge to the edge of the straight bit.

b. Mark the line to show you the distance from the guide's base to the fence. Afterwards, measure ¼" from the base to the waste side of this mark.

c. Adjust the height of the router bit to just a little deeper than the base's thickness. Clamp the guide to your sawhorses to prevent it from shifting. Now, hold the router base tight against the guide fence and then rout the router to smoothen the rough edge. And then, label the routed side and show what direction the router travelled.

d. Place the edges that you have placed the guide on near the edge of the piece you want to place glue on. Leave about 1/16" on the edge to serve as allowance for the router to cut on. Clamp the pieces in this position and then rout the board. If the table saw that you would be using can handle the piece that you want to use as a joint, put the routed edge against the fence of your tablesaw and then cut a straight parallel edge right on the opposite side. If your workpiece cannot fit in your table saw, reclamp the guide that you are using to rout the edge.

4. Making Mortise-and-Tenon Joints

Mortise-and-tenon types of joints are known to be one of the strongest joints that you can create in a woodworking project. They are ideal for making construction frames that need to be durable, which is why they are typically used in making chairs and tables.

Mortise-and-tenon joints come in different types:

a. Stopped/blind

b. Angled

c. Wedged

d. Through

While they are different, the method on how they are constructed is the same. All you need is to produce the mortise, or a piece of wood that accepts the tenon, and the tenon, which is a tongue-like construction at the end of a piece that fits right into the mortise.

The tenon can be made with a shoulder (the square notch before the tenon), or without it, depending on the design of the piece that you are trying to construct. However, a shouldered tenon tends to hide less right into the mortise compared to a perfect or unshoulderedone.

To create a stopped/blind mortise-and-tenon joint, or a joint wherein the tenon is fully hidden into the mortise, follow these steps:

a. Make a mark on your board to indicate where the mortise would go.

b. Select the mortising bit that is about the same width of the mortise. Make sure that the mortising bit doesn't go over it.

c. Position the workpiece carefully with a fence to make sure that the mark is right on the bit's position.

d. After setting the depth of cut, slowly drill into the workpiece. See to it that the first hole that you make is on one end of the mortise.

e. Drill another pass at the other end of the mortise.

f. Once you are done with the drilling, chisel or drill out the remaining wood on the mortise portion. You can clean up the hole using a chisel.

To create the tenon, follow these steps:

a. Mark the sides of the board that you want to turn into a tenon.

b. Set the depth of cut to match the thickness of the tenon.

c. Line up the cut and feed the wood through the saw using a miter gauge. Turn over the board to do the other side. Take note that you may need to make another pass if the tenon that you want to make is longer than the dado blade that you are using.

d. Clean up the tenon that you have done with the chisel.

If you want to construct a shoulder on the tenon, you can repeat these steps but put the board on the edge instead of its face.

5. Sharpening Your Tools

To make your woodshop safe and your tools effective, it is important that you keep the edges of your tools sharp. While there are many ways to sharpen your tools, you can follow these sharpening steps for beginners to help you get started on maintaining your tools. This method would only require you to have some waterstones, a jig, and a few minutes.

a. Achieve the flat back

While some of the blades that you have in your shop already come with a flat back, you would want to make sure that they are polished. To do that, place a magnet over the bevel to help you with your grip. Next, work on the back of the tool using a #1000-grit waterstone, and then follow it up with a #4000 stone. Finish the polishing with a #8000 stone. If you think that the back needs extra polishing, use an #80 sandpaper to finish the job.

b. Make sure that the bevel is square

If the primary bevel of your tool is not straight across a flat surface, regrind it using the earlier step.

c. Use the jig for the blade

Most blades would need a side-clamp honing guide, or a jig with a narrow wheel. Using this jig, you can use your finger to apply pressure when you want to hone the edge straight, or alternately use a slight camber. Afterwards, place the plane blade into the jig at about 30°.

d. Hone the secondary bevel straight

Use two fingers to apply pressure at the corner of the blade placed against a #1000-grit waterstone. Once you are in position, pull back the blade you intend to sharpen towards you about 10 times. After sharpening, feel the edge of the blade if it has burrs, or curled up metal normally caused by scratches on the metal. If burrs are present, continue honing the blade with a #4000-grit waterstone, and then finish off with an #8000-grit waterstone.

CHAPTER 8

Finish Right

Finishing your piece is not as complicated as you may think. While there are conditions that may create unexpected results in wood after using a particular use of stain or other finishing material, there are a lot of ways that would create a predictable outcome and prevent common finishing problems.

Here are some ways to get the right finishing results:

1. Study at least three types of finishes.

Why three? It is because you are not likely to build only one kind of project and use only one wood material. By learning other kinds of finishes, you can select the more appropriate finish for the material that you are working on.

For example, if you are building a Shaker-style piece, it would look marvelously if you apply an oil-based finish. However, an easy-to-apply oil finish would not work well with any project that works best with a film-building type of finish. You may want to use varnish, lacquer, polyutherane, or shellac on that kind of project instead.

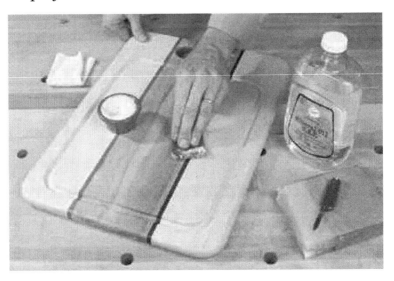

2. Color wood appropriately.

Learning how to color wood would also let you know that there are some dyes or stains that are more absorbent in certain kinds of wood. Wood stocks like walnut and mahogany are well-known for taking in stains and dyes evenly. However, you do not want to bury the wood's beautiful color with a dark stains – you would want to color the wood instead to enhance the grains and make the wood appear warmer. However, keep in mind that there are other fine wood types that would not soak in stains well.

3. Decide on the finish before you start the project.

Woodgrain Filler tinted with "Moorish Teak" oil stain | Tung Oil Varnish "wet-sanded" | Brown Maple dye, sealer, glaze with "Dark Walnut" gel stain

Make it a point to use the finishing style that you already know is best for the type of wood and the type of project. This would be helpful to consider if you want to keep your finished piece protected from scratches or moisture once you are already done with it.

4. Make samples.

Spend some time in making a sample board using the same wood material that you are to use in your project. When preparing a sample, make sure that you prepare the wood in the same way you are going to prepare it for your woodworking project. Sand the board using the same sandpaper grit that you intend to use, and then use finishing sandpaper afterwards. You can also decide to color a portion of the board if you think your project requires it. Dye or apply stain to a section of the wooden board, and then apply the topcoat. Doing so would allow you to take note of every finishing step and see how your project would look like. If you do not like what the board looked like, then you have an idea that the finishing ideas you have in mind is worth revising instead of sticking to. Making samples saves you from having a finished product ruined by a wrong type of finishing.

5. Sand in between coats.

If you want to produce a smooth finish, you would definitely want to sand in between finishing coats to remove those small imperfections or nibs that show up after applying a finishing layer. These nibs may be grains that stand out against the single coat applied, dust that have fallen into the wet finish, or air bubbles that have popped up when the finish dried out. It may also mean that the finish is not laid out smoothly on the wood.

You can sand dried finishing coats using a #240-grit stearated aluminum oxide paper, or sand a wet finish with a wet/dry sandpaper with #400 grit. To wet sand the finish, apply a few drops of liquid detergent to wet the finish.

CHAPTER 9

Troubleshooting Tips

Since you are starting out with handling projects, it is very likely that you would make a few mistakes and run into some problems. Don't worry – it is usual to run into some bumps, even for seasoned craftsmen. As long as you know how to troubleshoot and remedy common woodworking problems, you can still end up producing a good craft.

Here are some troubleshooting and repair tips that you can use:

1. Blotchy or uneven finish

You can end up having unsightly finish when you use stains or an oil finish. Blotches happen because of the pores in the wood or when you used different amounts of oil in certain parts of the piece. You would not be able to correct this error when it already happened, but there are two ways to avoid it in the future:

a. use pore-filling products or a sanding sealer to fill in the wood pores before you take care of the final finish

b. use a finish that is designed to sit on top of the wood, such as shellac or varnish.

2. Rocking tables

Most woodworkers deal with rocking tables, even after considerable experience in making furniture. The only culprit responsible for this is uneven table lengths, which can be easily avoided by cutting pieces with precise measurement. However, it can also happen when the wood moves after the table has been assembled.

To fix this problem after you have glued up your table, you can adjust the length of the table legs until it sits evenly on the floor. To do this, place the uneven table on a flat workbench and rock it until you spot which leg is the longest. Push that leg against the edge of the workbench and level the table to see how much you need to cut on the long leg. With your pocket or utility knife, score that point where the surface of the workbench crosses with the long leg. Sand or plane that leg to that mark.

3. Fuzzy surface after sanding

Some types of wood, like birch, can become fuzzy to the touch when you sand them too much. The reason is that the fibers of the wood break during sanding, which creates that hair-like appearance on the wood's surface. No matter what happens, do not stain a surface that still has fuzz.

If you are aware that the wood that you used tends to fuzz, use a sandpaper with lower grit, such as 120, and sand out the fur from the wood. Do not scrape them or use a fine paper when removing them.

4. Joints do not fit together well

It happens that even when you have taken the right measurements and cut the wood according to mark, joints do not fit that well against each other after gluing. If you experience this situation, it is possible that the joints are way too tight, or that you managed to pull the joints partway and have locked up.

See to it that you are avoiding tight joints by doing a dry fit first. You can pound the joints together using your mallet and if you fill that you need to exert too much effort to put them together, then that is a telltale sign that you need to loosen the parts first before applying glue. If you are trying to make a mortise-and-tenon joint, you may want to shave the tenon a bit until you are able to put the pieces together with minimal mallet tapping or by hand.

If you think that the joints have locked up in the middle of assembly, then you may need to pound it hard or use clamps to get the part moving again. However, depending on how locked up the parts are, it is possible that you may not get them to move. To avoid this situation, fully pull joints together when you try to assemble them. Avoid partially attaching joints – make sure that you attach the joint completely before you move on to another one.

5. Joints are too loose

If you are trying to make a mortise-and-tenon joint, a loose joint fit may become a huge problem in your piece, since the strength of the joint largely depends on how the tenon and the mortise sits against each other. Don't worry about it that much – instead of cutting a new tenon, you can adjust its size instead by using an epoxy resin glue to fill the gap. Epoxy resin glues are two-part glues that can be used to cure wood gaps since it expands when it dries. If you still do not trust the strength of the joint, you can use a piece of thin wood and glue it in to fill the gap in the tenon.

6. Wood splits while being sawed

A tear-out may happen when you run a piece of wood across the saw, which happens when the blade grabbed an unsupported wood edge as the board exits the saw. You would see tear-outs at the back edge of your stock.

To avoid this from happening, place a backing board against your stock's back edge whenever you make a cut in order for the backing board to get the tear-out instead. You can also avoid tear-outs if you do a crosscut before a rip cut, if you do not have a backing board available.

7. Tabletop is not flat

If you are certain that the wood that you have used for your tabletop has not warped, twisted, or cupped, the uneven table top is caused by any of the following: you applied too much clamp pressure when you glued the table pieces together, or the edges of the board are not perfectly square or straight.

If you need to make an uneven tabletop flat, your option is to plane the board and sand it until it becomes even. However, you may not want to go this way since it would reduce the thickness of the wood. Your better option is to cut the top from the joints and start over. You can avoid running into a similar problem by adjusting the jointer well to make sure that you are creating perfect square edges. Do not apply too much pressure on the clamps when you put the pieces together. You can avoid that by placing an additional clamp on top of the board.

CHAPTER 10

Sample Beginner Project

Now that you are familiarized with the wood and tools and have set up your very own workshop, it is time to set off on a couple of beginner projects. Shown here is an example of a beginner project that is simple and easy to finish for beginners.

Project #1 – Wooden Toolbox

This project is designed to familiarize you with the practice of working with woodworking tools. It's fairly straightforward and isn't too complicated

Tools required: Materials required:

Hand saw   One 1"x4"x8' wood board

Tape Measure   One 1"x2"x8' wood board

Marking instrument   1-pound box 1-3/8" ring shank drywall nails

C-Clamp

Drill with 5/64" bit

Step 1

First, mark each of the boards. Mark the 1"x2"x8' board every 12 inches. Mark the 1"x4"x8' board at the 12", 24", 36", 48", 60", 72", 82 and ½" and 93" marks.

Step 2

Cut the boards at the marked areas. The resulting parts that you need to build the toolbox are the following:

One 1"x2"x12" board to serve as the handle

Three 1"x4"x12" boards to serve as the toolbox sides

One 1"x4"x10½" board to serve as the toolbox bottom

Any rough edges resulting from cutting should be sanded.

Step 3

Cut one of the three 1"x4"x12" boards at the middle (6 inches from the edge) to serve as the tall sides of the toolbox.

Step 4

Mark and drill the pilot holes. Pilot holes for each of the sides should be as follows.

For the long sides: Two pilot holes each 4" inches from the edge lengthwise and two pilot holes 1 ½ inches from the edge crosswise.

For the handle: Two pilot holes on both ends, each ¾" inches from the edge crosswise and 3/8" inches from the edge lengthwise.

For the tall sides: Two pilot holes at the corners of one end, each 1 inch from the edge crosswise. Leave a little bit of space to serve as lengthwise distance from the edge, and make sure that it is equal for all pilot holes.

Since the boards are thin, it is best to clamp them together, marks aligned and drill them at the same time.

Step 5

Nail the whole thing together. Though not required, you can use a glue gun to hold the pieces in place while you hammer them together.

Place a nail in the hole of a tall side and hammer it into the bottom side. Do the same for the other tall side.

Afterwards, do the same with the long sides, nailing it into the bottom side following the pilot holes you drilled.

Finally, finish by nailing the handle on top of the tall sides.

Conclusion

I hope this book was able to help you to start out in the wonderful art of woodworking.

This book is meant to be a beginner's guide. Its aim is to familiarize you with the different tools and wood and to help you get started with woodworking. It is meant to nudge you into the right direction and show you what you should know up front should you desire to be a woodworker. There are a lot more things to learn about this craft, and this book is just one of those that provide you with useful information.

Remembering the basic guidelines of choosing wood, woodworking safety, and the different woodworking tools will help you to set upon the path of grander and more complex woodworking. Use this information, and keep on searching for things that can help you develop your skill so that you will become an accomplished woodcraftsman one day.

The next step is to keep on practicing your craft and develop your skill, and remember to invest adequate time and patience in this craft.

Would you do me a favor?

Finally, if you enjoyed this book, please take the time to share your thoughts and post a positive review on Amazon. It'd be greatly appreciated!

Thank you and good luck!

Made in the USA
San Bernardino, CA
06 August 2020